GETTING READY FOR
HEAVEN

A Believer's Guide to Final Affairs

How to be spiritually, personally, and legally ready
to leave for home!

by
Jan Irvin
Child of God

Table Of Contents

Introduction

On July 4th, 2017, at the ripe old age of 65, I was joyfully riding a bicycle, grilling dinner for family and otherwise celebrating the 4th of July. On July 5th, I woke up in a hospital bed wearing diapers and drinking chicken broth. It seems my appendix had other plans. Many in the medical community who reviewed my medical files after the ordeal looked at me in amazement and told me they were frankly flabbergasted that I had pulled through. So was I! I remember awakening after surgery and realizing that my body felt "DEAD"; totally non responsive, and I was thinking to myself very nonchalantly "Well, okay, I'm not going to survive this....so let's see....I've got my will, got my obituary written...got an insurance policy....hubby should be okay.....so alright, Jesus, if you are ready, I am!!" I then closed my eyes for what I was sure would be the last time.....

It was a slow go, but around 60 days later, I did finally regain my health back to 75% and I decided that I would indeed continue to live for a few more years, providing I don't step out in front of a bus. But it was scary. It made me start to think about life and health and such from a very different perspective.

My husband, the love of my life, was 72 at the time, and not doing very well in his battle with diabetes. Who knew

just how much longer he had as well? He has the best
care giver money can buy (me!) and I am determined
to keep him around for many more years yet, but there
are many factors beyond my control. Modern medicine
is truly miraculous, but every person is different in how
they respond to medications and also disease symptoms.
There simply are no guarantees in life. I know many who
didn't make it to 65, including my own parents!

I began to ask friends and family about their "final plans"
to help learn and find a starting place, and discovered that
most people do not want to even talk about the subject!
Most have no plans, because to have plans means there
has to be a recognition of the fact that the day will come
that they WILL die, and conversation about such things is
considered morbid, gross, depressing, negative, yucky,
etc. The average person procrastinates about planning
for this part of their life until the last minute when something happens, and there they are caught with "their funeral pants down", leaving all the final planning to the loved
ones who are already reeling from the grief and shock of
their passing. Not good.

I decided to not procrastinate; to do my "homework" and
have everything in order so that when that time comes
for me, all those tough decisions will have already been
made. I wanted to make a step by step "checklist", so
that when I fall off that mountain I'm trying to climb or
jump out of an airplane with a parachute that doesn't
work, a clear thinking friend (or my executor) can follow
the outline and get things taken care of as quickly and
painlessly (and cost effectively) as possible. Besides,
having been through the process of having to make these
decisions with my dad when my mom passed away un-

expectedly from a heart attack, I knew full well how tough it can be and I don't want to wish that on anyone else! How hard can it be, right? It couldn't take long! Just jump in there, find out what has to be done, write up a plan to throw in a file and call it done, right? Wrong! Wowza, there's a whole lot to be considered!!

Since most folks I asked what they had done for their own planning threw their hands in the air and ran away screaming something like "I don't want to talk about it!!!!!" I began to research on the internet to see what I could find. There are a few books out there, and they are helpful, but most are very "secular" in their views, many are overwhelming, and most were not"specific" enough for me, and so I found myself skipping over a lot of the material, looking for the real "meat" of what I needed to know. I called a few funeral homes and asked them questions, as well. I could "hear" them smiling as I asked them questions about death and burials. They LOVED talking to me about it, but still, they did not have all the answers. I talked to my attorney, my accountant, a financial planner and two pastor friends trying to find answers, but only found bits and pieces. After several people replied to me that they were also clueless about what needed to be done and asked if I would share with them what I learned, I decided I would write a short book about it. Understand that I am NOT an attorney. I am a small business owner with a retirement villa waiting for me with Jesus, and I hope that this guide may assist you in tackling this tough subject and getting your affairs in order. You will most likely need the guidance of a qualified attorney or financial planner as you work your way through this. I am going to try to keep it short and to the point, but be aware it will totally be from a Christian perspective. There's no way

I can have the answers to every possible question/scenario, but hopefully I will be able to point you in the right direction in most matters.

Getting Ready Ahead of Time

I feel that there are 3 basic areas where you need to be prepared ahead of time. Let's face it, preparing for these things while you are clear thinking and can address it in a serious, albeit light hearted manner is certainly a lot easier! This is, after all, a huge step in your life, and one that WILL happen, sooner or later. In fact, since it does require so much attention to detail, it's a huge job just to dump at the feet of your loved ones! (Particularly when they are already really stressed out!) As a person who loves Christ and believes His promises are absolutely positively true, I face my own demise with excitement and anticipation. In my view, it is a bigger event than birth, graduation, marriage, or your basic barmitzvah. So if you are serious about getting this done and out of the way, let's get down to addressing those areas: how to be ready spiritually, personally and legally.

Getting Ready Spiritually

First you have to understand and accept that you WILL die. A quote I saw on the internet lately read:

> "How can we seek a safe Christian walk when the core principle of our faith requires death? Someone had to die, and we have to die."

There is no other way to get to heaven, where our Master is!

Personally, I have no fear of death. I fear how ("the process"), I will die, but not THAT I will die. I know where I am going and am excited about it! I truly believe that when I am drawing my last breath I will feel like a kid on Christmas Eve, full of anticipation and excitement! I will soon be seeing all my old friends and family, even my beloved pets, and most of all, finally, my Lord and Savior! WOW! I'm not one who thinks of my impending eventual death with remorse or "oh no" in my head. The Bible describes death as going to your "reward" and even says you should celebrate and rejoice when a person dies, if they were a believer!

I find it somewhat strange, actually, that believers would be so filled with dread and want to avoid the topic of their eventual death. After all, isn't this the whole basis of

Christianity? That Christ died on the cross for us and in doing so, long story short, gives us the promise of ever lasting life in heaven with HIM? If that is not true, then the whole basis of Christianity is gone! And I have heard that there are those who have apprehensions concerning heaven; that it will be boring and monotonous; that you will float around on a cloud strumming a harp and singing hymns forever. Do you really think that the place where the Lord of this universe lives would be like that?? In my view, death and going to Heaven is what all Christians should long for, wait for, and is what this whole life is about while you are here! While admittedly the "process" of how you get from here to heaven is a bit unnerving, being at home in Heaven with Jesus is what we all look forward to! In fact, the older you get, the more you will re-alize that this earth is not your home; you are only visiting!

If you really don't think you can get past your anxiety about your eventual death, then I highly recommend that you read the book "Heaven" by Randy Alcorn or "A Place Called Heaven" by Robert Jeffress. These books will totally change your mind!! No, you won't float around on a cloud strumming a harp and singing hymns forever. No, you won't just stand around with your hands in your robe pockets. Life in Heaven is not a lot different from what we know as life now, but remove the bad stuff; the "sin" fac-tor. I know, hard to imagine, right?? Scripture does con-tain a lot of references to Heaven, and Randy Alcorn does a great job in bringing them to light. Jesus talks about Heaven a lot, but Hell even more! You might want to do some research on both of these places!

To be spiritually ready, you have to be on good terms with the realization that you WILL die someday. As my dear old mom used to say "There's not one of us who is going to get out of this thing alive….". I would think that for an atheist, this would be a tough pill to swallow and especially hard on their family members. Once old Joe passes away, he's gone forever, right? No, as a Christian, I don't believe that for a minute!

When you get "spiritually ready", you will want to pack your "spiritual" bags. Make sure you are right with everyone possible. Give forgiveness freely with lots of hugs! Listen for the Lord's voice and any opportunity to put some points on the scoreboard for Him before you leave here! If you are a Christian, then I'm sure I'm "preaching to the choir", here, but you get my drift! Of course, you should practice this regularly, not just at the last minute because you think you are about to leave this earth!!

> "To be absent from the body is to be present with the Lord." 2 Corinthians 5:8

Do you believe that?? I have to ask that question, because if you truly are a believer then your impending death should not shake you to the core as it does non believers. Again, the whole premise of Christianity is based around the fact that Christ really was who He said He was - the Son of God, and that He really did rise from the grave and ascend into Heaven.

> "And If I go and prepare a place for you, I will come back and take you to be with me that you may also be where I am." John 14:3

WOW! So do you believe that the promises of Jesus are true??

In my opinion, this is the biggest event you will experience in your life! The moment you take your last breath here, you will be headed to your new forever home! It's hard to conceive! A home where there's plenty of delicious, wonderful food that's all healthy for you! Your loved ones are there and they are sweeter and nicer than they ever could have been here! The whole place smells like gardenias, honeysuckle and roses! It is my firm belief that even your beloved pets will greet you as well! And most of all, you will at last get to meet face to face, up close and personal, our Lord and Savior! I cannot wait to get to hug Him!!

If you have ever been through a major airport, you are familiar with the moving sidewalks available to help you speedily navigate across large areas to get to your gate. You can "power walk" down those and really cover some ground, but when you come to the end of it, you'd better be ready to step off of it with all your bags and your body fully balanced or it can throw you for a loop! Quite embarrassing! If that sounds like the "voice of experience".... well.... probably.... I'm admitting nothing. I can envision that moving sidewalk being our life here on earth. It goes by fast! And when you get to the end – and you can usually see it coming – you need to be able to hand your bags off to the folks behind you and make that step onto the new ground as smoothly as possible. Once you step off the sidewalk, your life does not end, but you now exist in a new realm, unseen by those still in the airport!

As a science major, I feel compelled to also throw in just a smidgin of science that backs up creation. It has been proven many years ago that "Energy is neither created nor destroyed, only changed". WE ARE ENERGY. We consist of a vibrational pattern, and each of us has a pattern that is truly unique; just as there are no two snow-flakes alike. God created all these vibrational patterns in Genesis, by His very voice (the WORD) speaking the sound waves into existence. God knows each of us by our vibrational pattern. He knows when we are stressed, happy, etc., by our pattern. He knows when every sparrow falls by their pattern. Over 50 years ago at this writing, the Russians discovered Kirlian Photography, (high voltage electrophotography) which is a special type of photography which captures the "aura", or vibrations, of living creatures. In countless studies, this photography has shown over and over again the vibrational image of a soul (energy) leaving the body upon death! I also know a few people who visibly witnessed this phenomenon with their own eyes!! When our physical body dies, our energy lives on ---- somewhere! There is so much more I could say here, but don't get me started!

Personally, I think that in most cases the reason people are anxious about dying is because despite how ravaged our physical body may be with disease and/or old age, our "soul" (or "vibrational energy") is still functioning perfectly (remember that we were made "fearfully and wonderfully") and instinctively knows that we will continue to exist despite what happens to the failing body. It's difficult for our human minds to comprehend how we will continue to exist without our body, and how we will make the transition. So often as we watch our body fail, doctors shaking their heads and relatives gathering, our mind says "But I'm fine! I'm still me!! This can't be all there is!" Indeed, this life here truly isn't "all there is"!

One other note here is that if you fear the "process" of how you will leave this earth, realize you do have some control over it. If you don't want to die of cancer, don't smoke. That's the single leading cause of cancer. If you don't want to die of diabetes, Alzheimer disease, heart disease and a myriad of other intestinal and digestive related issues and other cancers, then don't let carbs, alcohol and junk food control your life. Our "Standard American Diet" (SAD) is killing us, but that's a whole separate topic! Of course, there are no guarantees in life, regardless of your diet and lifestyle, but avoiding or at least limiting these things can definitely lead to a healthier existence while you are here!

Thinking outside of our limited physical environment tied mind is extremely difficult. Of course it has been proven many years ago that there are parts of the light spectrum we cannot see, and parts of the sound spectrum we cannot hear. Most of it! So that tells you there is a lot that goes on that you cannot see or hear; a very large "spiritual" universe! I truly hope you can address this whole preparation for your "metamorphosis" with a big smile and no stress! If you TRULY know where you are going, it shouldn't be hard to do!

Getting Ready Personally

In my opinion, the main reason you need to do all this is to make it as easy as possible on the ones you leave behind. That's what it's all about! The more you have already planned, the easier it is for them! Nobody actually wants to have to come up with your eulogy, obituary, music, etc. Of course, you may also like the satisfaction of knowing that the things and possessions you had here on earth will be distributed as you would wish, and not just carted off to Good Will or given to that no good son in law.

On the morning of February 28, 1979, I got my usual 7:30 am call from my dad. It was almost a ritual he had established. I would answer the phone to hear him say "Have I told you I love you today?" I would respond with a laugh, "No, dad, not yet!" and he would say "Well, I love you today!! Bye!" But on this morning when I answered, he didn't speak for a few seconds. Finally, when he did, it was to say "Your mother has died this morning….." My mother was 51 years old and 98 pounds, a smoker (trying hard to quit) who had just been put on HRT (Hormone Replacement Therapy). At that time they did not know that you can't put a smoker on HRT; it causes massive blood clots. She was one of the statistics that taught them that. To put it mildly, this was NOT something we were expecting!!

Within a couple of days after this, I made the hasty decision to get most of her stuff out of the house; particularly stuff from the bedroom (clothes) that would make my dad grieve when he looked at it. I recruited a cousin to help me, and we got it all out of there in short order and carried it to Good Will. At the time, I felt good about doing it because it did help my dad, and he was the one suffering the most. A few years later though, I reflected back on that decision and wished I had kept some of her clothes or other trinkets for myself as a memory of her. I was only thinking of my dad at the time. Since then I have decided that if I ever again find myself having to help another person quickly clean things out (which is common practice), I would recommend that everything is boxed up and put into storage for one year. After that year, unpack everything and make logical decisions what to do with it.

Many years ago, a long time friend of my husband passed away. Her husband had died several years prior to this, and her daughter asked my husband and I to assist her in cleaning out her mother's house so she could put it on the market. She wanted it all gone, not just packed up as I suggested. It was an experience I will never forget. Fifty or more years of living in this house meant every nook and cranny, every drawer, every cabinet and closet was filled to the brim. I remember feeling overwhelmed at the thought of having to carefully go through such a huge mountain of what were precious possessions of this family, sorting out what to keep and what to give away and what to trash. It was a huge job that you can't approach in any way other than with respect and dignity. As I sorted through a kitchen "junk drawer" like all us women have, the picture of someone having to do this at my house hit my brain! Oh my goodness! Yes, inevitably this job would fall to someone to do at my own home! I vowed right then that I would do whatever it took to take away as much of this job as possible in the future. But how??

Downsizing

After my appendectomy scare, that junk drawer of mine looked rather ominous. There it was, reminding me that someone may soon have to deal with it! I began to look through my house and realized what a huge collection of "stuff" we had accumulated over the years. One bedroom closet served as my sewing room. When was the last time I had touched that sewing machine? Over 15 years, no doubt! I used it constantly when the kids were grow-ing up, but not so much anymore….. An inventory of the kitchen revealed lots of small appliances and gadgets of all kinds, also not used in years….. a stroll through the library revealed lots of books, the tops covered in dust as they sat on the shelf, long ago read and then filed away not to be thought of again. DVDs and Video cassettes of old movies, and did I mention tons of Christmas dec-orations I no longer had the energy to put out?? Again I envisioned people going through my house, shaking their heads and conversing about what in the world they would do with all this STUFF, and the hours and even days it would take to deal with it all! What if they threw away some of the "good" stuff someone else could really use!?!?! And then I got an idea!

Instead of waiting to let friends and relatives (who proba-bly already have their own house full of "stuff") have this chore, why not hand select who I wanted to receive it? Why not sort out the "trash" myself, pick out cherished or useful items I don't use anymore and give them away my-self, in that way knowing it is used and appreciated and I get to see the smile and get the hugs and thank-yous NOW? I call it "Downsizing"!

I went through our clothes closets and was amazed at how many clothes I found that neither of us wore any-more; wrong style – no lets be honest – wrong SIZE..... and was proud to donate them to a women's shelter to help raise money for their assistance! Dusty kitchen ap-pliances went to homeless shelters who could use them in the kitchen or a young couple just starting out in life and on a limited income. This was fun! I have decided that about every 5 years I will weed out my house and give away things as I please, leaving less to be dealt with in the end and most of all getting to see those smiles and get the hugs for helping folks in the process!

I'm not saying this is something you MUST do, but you may want to consider it. It will give you a tremendous amount of satisfaction!

DRASTIC Downsizing!

Here is one other consideration on downsizing, and a serious one to think over. After studying all about the ins and outs of the legal aspects of death, I now understand why so many seniors sell out, buy a motor home and tour the country! The less your assets and worth at the time of your death, the simpler it is for everyone and a lot cheaper as well. The idea is to have nothing left to fight over! (Or go through probate!) Depending on your situa-tion, your age at the time of your spouse's death, etc., you may want to consider drastic downsizing. Here are some options:

Sell out your estate/home and buy an RV, motor home or "tiny house" to live in, putting the cash from your estate in your account to ensure you have ample funds to live your remaining years in comfort, doing whatever you want to do. Or move in with a relative or friend and split the costs. Go economy!

Donate your house to your favorite church, charity, Christian school, etc. This would allow you to remain in your residence until your demise, but would tie up the funds it would bring in if sold, so be sure you have enough money in the bank to take care of your needs before you go this route.

Sign your home over to whoever it is you wanted to have it (child, grandchild, etc). This also SHOULD allow you to remain in your home until your demise; but be careful here. Sometimes those sweethearts can get anxious/ greedy. You will need to check with an attorney on this, because it must be done within a number of years (5 to 7) before you might end up needing a nursing home, in which case the state may step in and take possession of your home to go towards your bills. Normally they won't do this unless the entire estate is worth around 75K or more, however.

Do a reverse mortgage. This allows you to stay in your home and get paid while doing it. Investigate the companies that offer this thoroughly and understand what you are getting into before signing on the dotted line!

Gifting

Gifting is a way to disperse your assets to your children, grand children, a charity, etc. You will need to talk to a good financial adviser about this, as there are a lot of different ways to go and dollar amounts you will need to be aware of in order to do this with the smallest amount of tax penalty.

Currently, according to my accountant, you can "gift" up to $15,000 each to as many donees as you like, per year. This means a husband and wife can gift $30,000 to various donees per year. Again, I highly advise that you speak to a financial expert about this.

Payable on Death Bank Accounts

This is a special account that you will have to go to the bank and set up. You will have to fill out a form naming who you want to inherit the money in your account after your death. Not to worry, for as long as you live that person you named will have no rights to this money and you can go in and change it to someone else if you need to. Otherwise, you use your account as you normally would. At your death, the beneficiary you name will be able to collect whatever is in the account after showing proper ID as to who they are. If your account is set up in this way, it will not be included in probate. Be aware, however, that states that have estate/inheritance taxes may be able to claim some of these proceeds. The bank may need to know those taxes were paid before they will release the money.

Retirement Accounts

You can put money in a retirement account (IRA/401(k)) and name a beneficiary to this account, and this will not have to go through probate, either. The beneficiary can claim the money through the custodian.

Transfer-on-Death Deeds for Real Estate (TODD)

Although this can't be done in every state, in the ones that do allow it (Alaska, Arizona, Arkansas, California, Colorado, District of Columbia, Hawaii, Illinois, Kansas, Minnesota, Missouri, Nebraska, Nevada, New Mexico, North Dakota, Ohio, Oklahoma, Oregon, South Dakota, Texas, Virginia, Washington, West Virginia, Wisconsin and Wyoming), you can transfer real estate using one of these deeds, and it will not require probate. Make sure the deed states clearly that it doesn't take effect until your death (don't worry you can change it at any time), and also make sure it is signed, notarized, and filed as any official deed would be. There is a lot of information available on the internet about this topic.

Internet Definition of TODD:
A transfer-on-death(TOD) deed, or beneficiary deed, allows an owner of real property to execute a deed that names a beneficiary who will obtain title to the property at the owner's death without going through probate.

Bottom Line: my advice is, if you are up in years and your spouse dies, start liquidating assets! Set you sights on where you want to end up that's economical for you – a "Dell Webb", a cabin on the beach, an RV, or a bedroom in the kid's house. If there's not much of your estate left when you check into your permanent retirement home, it's so much simpler for everyone concerned! Again, talk to your attorney and/or financial adviser. There are many many different ways of gifting, disposing of property and arranging trusts/wills.

Details, details, details….

There are many things you will need to think about when getting ready personally. More than I ever dreamed! The more of this you can do NOW, the easier it will be for all concerned when that time comes!

I suggest you make a list of the following miscellaneous information:

- Id's and passwords necessary for social media, bank accounts, credit card accounts, email address-es, social media, etc.
- Any information regarding insurance policies (policy number, expiration date, who to contact)
- What credit cards or loans are in your name that will need to be closed/paid? (These can be very difficult; if at all possible, close them ahead of time!)
- Any information regarding a safe deposit box or oth-er assets that might be "out of sight/out of mind"
- Any information on real estate or other capital items that are in your name
- Where exactly is that glass jar buried in the back yard that has the family fortune in it?

Who To Notify

This is a bigger "undertaking" than you realize. You most

likely have more friends and relatives than you realize who would be offended if they weren't notified. Why not take the time to list all these folks and have their contact information handy?? Usually just a valid phone number is adequate. You may want a comment on your Facebook page, as well, to let a large number of folks know what's going on. If you do, you will need to be sure the Executor knows your log in ID and password.

Your Eulogy

When your friends and relatives gather to pay their last respects, this will be most likely one of the last times they will ever hear anything much about you. What do you want them to know? Do you really want to leave this up to one of your close, grief stricken friends or relatives? Your speakers, particularly your pastor, will need to know "the basics" of your life. Who knows that better than you? What events in your life stand out? Remember that the goal, (in my opinion) of this whole funeral thing is to give your friends and loved ones "closure"; to make things easier on them. In my opinion, that means leaving them with comforting thoughts, funny memories, and most of all some kind of statement of your faith and how you think you will be feeling and what you will be doing while they are wiping their noses and sobbing. Can you cheer them up and make them know all is well?? This is your chance to help them with what you say here. You may even con-sider making a recording of your voice, telling them your-self what you want them to know. Or leaving a personal note to a spouse or your kids.

Your Obituary

Again, what do you want to say here? I recommend you have control of this and write your own, unless you are comfortable with the basic, plain vanilla type. In my experience, the folks reading it in the paper want to know more than the just the basics. Most obituaries I read in the paper make my nose curl up. They lack adequate information. This is YOUR experience! Take charge!! How about the picture that will be posted of you with the obit? Who do you want to pick that out?? I suggest you pick out your own!

Music Selections

Music is a staple at any type of funeral. Again, you need to choose your favorites. The more decisions you can make for yourself rather than leaving them to your executor or survivors, the less stressful it is for them! Music can have a strong effect and really leave a "final message", so carefully consider what you choose and the message it brings!

We had named a young man we love as a son to be our "alternate executor." He gladly accepted the job. One day not long after asking him to take on this dubious honor, he came to my house and asked me "Okay, since I'm going to be the Executive Vice President of your Will, do I get to pick any of the music?" It took me a moment to figure out what he had just said. "Alternate Executor, and no, the music will already be picked. Why? Did you have something in mind?" He excitedly said "YES!! For your husband, I know I have never been in his shop in all the

years I have known you guys that he didn't play 'Comfortably Numb' at least once! I know that's his favorite song!!
And besides, when your dead, you're.....comfortably numb!" I loved it, and hubby and I both agreed that perhaps we might throw "Comfortably Numb" in there somewhere. Obviously, it's best if you pick your own music, though!

The Funeral Itself

Do you have a burial policy or bottomless pockets? How do you want to be remembered? This will be a big determining factor in how you decide to wrap things up and bring "closure" to your friends and family. There are a lot of choices and decisions to be made here. Again, I remember going to the funeral home with my dad to make arrangements for my mother. NOT FUN! If you wait until something happens and then are forced to make these decisions while under probably the greatest grief you will experience in your life, it's fair to say that your choices may not be the best! And you may not even realize it until you get the final bill! No one is thinking clearly at a time like this, that's for sure!

So, what is to become of the body? There are many choices now as to what becomes of your body other than traditional embalming:

- Donation to a medical school
- Donation to a forensics school
- Shot into space
- Frozen (Cryogenics)
- Cremation

In most cases if you select one of these alternatives to traditional embalming, you will need to do so in advance. My husband and I chose to be donated to Southwest School of Medicine, and we are "card carrying members," so to speak. We are on their list and there are certain steps to be followed in the event of our death. Most local funeral parlors are familiar with this. For example, upon our death, simply call the local funeral parlor and they will come get the body and hold it for the school to come pick up from them. (Trust me, this is WAY desirable over you holding it yourself until the school can get there). This may cost about $200. That's it. No charges from the school. But realize these are not choices you can make at the last minute. If you don't chose an alternative and get it taken care of ahead of time, then you may be forced to go the traditional route. Also, a medial school will not take your body if you are mangled badly in a car wreck, burned up in a house fire or any other fun way to go. You will need to have alternative instructions in this event. If you donate your body, ask them what restrictions they have, if any.

Realize that if you die at home, a JP or coroner will have to issue a "death certificate" before much can be done. Also, as things are constantly changing, you can go on line and get it yourself. You will need the information off the deceased birth certificate to do this. It is issued by the Department of State Health Services Vital Statistics. It can be ordered online or from the county clerk's office. The online address for Texas is tx-dps.com. (Tip: Get several copies of the death certificate. I have been told by those who have already been through this to get at least 10-12 copies. The first copy is the most expensive, about $50, and any others you get at that same time are very cheap.

But if later you find you need another, it will be at the cost of that first expensive one again. Good advice!) If death occurs in a hospital, they may have staff on hand to take care of this, but remember to ask for multiple copies!

A word about caskets: you would be amazed at what you can find on the web! Environmentally friendly "pods" that deteriorate over time, caskets that look like beer cans, cars, etc., you name it. Pretty pricey, too! Additionally, if you are cremated, instead of having your ashes returned in an urn, you can now have your ashes fashioned into a diamond or any number of other things. This information is also readily available on the internet.

Remember: what becomes of your physical body after you depart from it does not matter. It will go back to ashes/dirt one way or the other over time, and you will be getting a new, resurrected body that although will look like you, will not age and break down over time!

Wakes/Memorials/Celebrations of Life/ Traditional/Visitations

There needs to be some type of "get together" shortly after you "relocate" in order to allow your friends and family to have "closure" regarding your departure. Traditionally this is all part of the basic funeral package and if that's what you have in mind, that's fine. There are options, however. Some may be far less costly.

Personally, the more "traditional" funerals I have attended, the more they left me cold. Something about the organ music calls to mind Bella Legosi and horror classics. My heart believes this should be a CELEBRATION of this person who had a life here on earth and now, as a Christian, they are in their new home with Jesus and all their family. This is what Jesus has promised us and what we all look forward to as the greatest hope that Christians have, right? So why all the long faces and "woe is me" music?

A "Celebration of Life" is becoming more and more popular. With this type of service, the person's life is celebrated typically by the showing of pictures from the time the person was born up until the final years. The pictures show major events such as special birthdays, lifetime friends, high school and/or college graduation, marriage, birth of kids, grandkids, etc. Normally while these pictures are being shown, music will be playing in the background. This music can vary in theme but normally is music religious in nature. I highly recommend that you sort through all your old pictures and select which ones you want to be used. There are places that will scan these pictures to a thumb drive or DVD, along with your selected music so that it is all ready to go when the big moment comes and one less thing for your loved ones to deal with. (Your local undertaker will probably be able to point you in the right direction for this if they don't provide the service themselves.) Be aware, however, that this is a pretty pricey service and will run you $250 to $375, depending on how many pictures and how many songs. I was told these average 30 pictures per song, and you will no doubt want 3-5 songs, depending on the presentation chosen. Typical price is $2.50 per picture, so you do the math here......

If you are handy with a computer, I researched this on the

web and found a program called "Smilebox" that will help you do it yourself if you are half way computer literate. Additionally, Walmart will scan 165 pictures for $25.00 to a dvd or USB, which is only 0.15 each if you send them in. Do you really need more than 165 pictures??? They also have scanners in the photo department where you can scan them yourself; as many as you want, for $3.00 per CD that they are scanned to. From here, you can transfer them using "Smilebox" or the like and join them with your music on a dvd/cd.

Again, you will know better than anyone else which moments and events in your life you want to "showcase", and perhaps the ones you'd just as soon leave out. I can't stress enough here that the idea is to make those left behind feel more comfortable about the situation and most of all to use your enthusiasm for living with Christ in Heaven to help take away their own fears and apprehensions, as well as to possibly sway some non believers in the crowd to take a second look at Jesus and what He offers!!

Epitaphs and Headstones

If you go the traditional route, a headstone will have to be selected. These can vary greatly on price, depending on size, inscription, and the amount of carving and "ornateness" to it. This can also be very stressful for the surviving family to have to deal with. Please have this already done if this is the way you are going to go. Contact your local funeral parlor or a monument company for details and pricing.

Many people like some sort of "epitaph" on their head-stone. Of course, if I were to have a headstone I would want people to laugh when they read it, and so I would go with something like "I told you I was sick". Again, this is something that needs lots of thought and planning ahead of time.

What do you want to leave close friends/family to remember you by?

Regardless of the type of funeral you plan; whether traditional or a Celebration, it's nice to leave your loved ones something to remember you by. A favorite cousin of mine had a baby oak tree available in a small container for anyone who wanted it. Personally, I will leave a copy of my autobiography and my favorite praise music on a jump drive for anyone who wants it. I plan to have maybe 3 copies readily available.

Many times people leave a hand written letter to their loved ones, or maybe even a recording of their voice speaking to them. This is also very nice, but must be done well in advance and adequate instructions left with it so it gets to the right people.

Personally, my goal is that people leave my "Celebration" in an "uplifted" and "happy" mental state. I want them to have no doubt as to what "retirement home" I went to, and hopefully create in them the desire to also put their name on that reservation list. For me, there will be no black attire allowed, and I hope the arrangement of activities I have in mind will leave everyone smiling when it's over.

Getting Ready Legally

In doing my research, I read somewhere that nearly 80% of people die "intestate". No will, no trust, nothing! WOW! Really? Of course some of this is due to unexpected or sudden deaths, but still, 80% is a huge number! Why? I believe the number one reason is procrastination. Nobody wants to deal with the inevitable and they keep putting it off. But another part of it is fear of the unknown.

Okay, you have to realize, as frank as this sounds, that once you pass away the buzzards will start to circle! Everyone will want a piece of what you had! If you are not legally prepared, the government and other agencies will end up with a large portion of what you have worked all your life for. This is not a fun thing to do and it can be expensive, but it can't be overlooked!!

Wills vs Trusts – The "Nitty Gritty"

So what about the legalities of death? You have the choice of three situations: a will, a trust, or nothing. The latter means you died without anything- neither a will nor a trust (known as "intestate"). This is not (NOT) the way to go! Many times this happens because "I'm too young to die...I've got plenty of time to make arrangements...I don't care what happens to my stuff or my family...I don't want to talk about it"! I remember my dad hated the thought of death and funerals and did not want to even talk about them. He used to say "The only funeral I plan to go to is mine and I may not show up for it!" He died intestate, but my mother had already passed, he had remarried, and his new wife and her 5 kids made sure they got everything of what little he had. I wish I would have known a little bit about how all this worked back then.....but it's history, now.

You must have a Last Will or Trust in place, or the state will end up deciding what happens to your stuff. Your heirs won't like this a bit, and if you were around to know what all happens, you would be fuming, yourself. These things are tricky and can be costly, and you need a good attorney and/or financial adviser that you know you can trust to do this. Most people go with a Last Will; but if you have property and such that values over $500,000 or more, a Trust might be the best way to go. Your attorney can explain the differences to you. (You might also take a look at "Legal Zoom" for assistance with this.) With a Trust, you more or less pay your probation fees up front as the attorney "funds" your trust. There's a lot of red tape in making sure all your assets are protected and go to the right places. If you are like me and just one of the "common folks", a Last Will should suffice. Just make sure you have one or the other.

Since you don't want to die "intestate", that leaves the first two, either a will or trust. In spite of what you may have heard, there are significant differences. A will is usually drawn by an attorney with you stating what you want to happen in the body of the instrument when it is drawn up. This may be amended later by you and your attorney.

Upon your demise, in order to legally transfer ownership of your assets to your heirs (i.e. cars, money, house/real estate, stocks and other items) your attorney will begin probation proceedings (which are usually lengthy...sometimes a year or more), during which time your heirs are left on hold, yet are responsible for interim legal fees and your ongoing credit responsibilities, which could be substantial.

Holographic Will

Most states will still honor what is called a "Holographic Will". As of this writing, the states that will honor it are: Alaska, Arizona, Arkansas, California, Colorado, Idaho, Kentucky, Louisiana, Maine, Michigan, Mississippi, Montana, Nebraska, Nevada, New Jersey, North Carolina, North Dakota, Oklahoma, Pennsylvania, South Dakota, Tennessee, Texas, Utah, Virginia, West Virginia and Wyoming.

The major requirement found throughout holographic will statutes is that a holographic will must be written entirely in the handwriting of the testator. Probate courts will not accept a typewritten will as a holographic will. In the case of a purported holographic will that is both typed and handwritten, such as a stationary will form that has been filled out, a probate court will typically ignore the typewritten provisions. The signing of a holographic will does not need to be witnessed, although some states require the holographic will to be dated. However, for admission to probate, a holographic will generally requires at least two individuals to testify that the holographic will was written in the handwriting of the decedent.

A Word About Probate

Four Basic Steps to Probate:
- Filing of a petition giving notice to heirs and beneficiaries
- Notice to all creditors and inventory of estate property
- Payment of all debts and taxes from the estate
- Any property is transferred according to the will

Trusts

A trust is quite different. Instead of drawing up a will, your attorney will draw up a Certificate of Trust. This creates a new legal entity that holds your assets in a trust that you control. To get your assets into this new instrument, you will "fund" the trust, and the trust will hold title to your items (car title, deeds, etc.) This terminology may seem difficult to understand, but what it means, literally, is that you change the name on the titles to your assets (home, property, automobiles, etc.) to the name of the TRUST instead of your name. In essence, the "Trust" now owns these items instead of you. This takes some time and must be carefully done. A common mistake people make when they do a trust is failing to change the titles into the name of the trust. If you don't "fund" the trust, it is a worthless piece of paper!

You administer the trust yourself. Typically, the trust is identified by something like "The John Doe Family Trust". Your assets are in the trust, but you retain control until your death, then a person previously named in the trust (normally your spouse) will administer the proceeds as you wished. Main advantage of a trust: saving the time and COST of probate. Try to find an attorney with lots of experience writing trusts.

Lady Bird Deeds

As of this writing, Lady Bird Deeds are only available in Texas, Florida, Michigan, Vermont and West Virginia. The beauty of the Lady Bird Deed is that it is a way to avoid probate without sacrificing control during your life. It is like a "life estate" in that the person who creates the deed transfers the property to himself for his lifetime, but then names one or more people, trusts, organizations, etc., who will inherit the property after the death of the original owner.

The good thing is that the original owner of this deed can change their mind about without involving the beneficiaries; in other words, you can still sell it, gift it, or whatever, without any involvement of anyone you named as beneficiaries.

The biggest value of a Lady Bird Deed, in my opinion, is that it is not considered a transfer of property and therefore will not be a penalty period where Medicaid calculations are concerned, avoiding loss of control of your property in Medicaid Recovery. It is definitely worth looking into if you live in a state where it is applicable!

As I mentioned earlier, the simplest thing to do is to have already distributed your assets to those you want to have them before you leave this place! The more you still have in your name, the bigger the problems and the more costly it is to legally disperse them.

Probate can be a real pain. This is the process of gathering up all the assets of a person to get titles changed, make sure your taxes and debts are paid, and otherwise distributing your possessions according to your will/trust. Depending on how many assets are involved, this can drag on for months and even years, being quite expensive.

The Internet is very helpful answering your questions... this can be very important to your heirs to save as much of the estate as possible. Generally, since there is no probate after your death, a trust properly drawn can be settled in a day (hours).

Most couples go with what is commonly called a "love nest" will or trust. In this situation, when a spouse dies, the remaining spouse now has legal possession of all assets with little cost or difficulty, whether the instrument in place was a will or a trust. The remaining spouse will now have the dubious honor of dispersing everything when they now change the existing will/trust to reflect their wishes now that they are the sole heir. This is where it can get very complicated if children, particularly step children are involved, if there are multiple marriages, etc. Then there is addressing the rare possibility that you and your spouse leave this earth at the same time.. now what?? In these situations, seek the advise of a GOOD attorney!!

Personal Memorandum – You Really Can't Take It With You

NOTE: My "spirit man" told me not long ago that there's a reason "you can't take it with you"....and that is because you totally won't WANT all this earthly junk in your new home! It doesn't belong there and what Jesus has waiting for you is so much better! So smile as you get rid of it!! Nothing down here matters! NOTHING!!!

This can be a difficult thing to grasp for some people. You work all your life to accumulate "stuff", be it real estate, cash, investments, household items, etc., only to find in your old age that you now must address getting rid of it all! To be honest, the thought that eventually someone else will be walking around in and living in the house my husband and I built and paid for and lived in 35+ years – OUR house-- seems rather odd, but is inevitable! I can just hear them in town "Yeah, we bought the old Irvin place...." It will happen!

Younger folks reading this may want to keep this in mind as they make their purchases and journey through life. Jesus says:

> "Lay not up for yourselves treasures upon earth, where moth and rust doth corrupt, and where thieves break through and steal: But lay up for yourselves treasures in heaven, where neither moth nor rust doth corrupt, and where thieves do not break through nor steal: For where your treasure is, there will your heart be also."
> Matthew 6:19-21

So, to help address this, you will need a "Personal Memorandum", a document that you make out that specifies who gets what. I have been told by my very efficient attorney that it does not even have to be notarized, but is 99.9% of the time honored and your wishes carried out. Just type it up and sign it, and put a copy with your legal documents.

Definitions

Some definitions you need to know:

Power of Attorney
A general power of attorney gives broad powers to a person or organization (known as an agent or attorney-in-fact) to act in your behalf. These powers include handling financial and business transactions, buying life insurance, settling claims, operating business interests, making gifts, and employing professional help.

Living Will/Last Will
A Living Will allows you to have a say in the type of health care treatment you receive should you find yourself unable to act for yourself. A Living Will is also commonly known as a Health Care Directive. You will need this if you find yourself in a situation where you are terminally ill/bed ridden. A Living Will deals with the type of health care treatment you will receive while alive. In contrast, a Last Will determines how your estate will be dispersed after you pass. Both documents are part of a strong estate plan.

Medical Power of Attorney

A Medical Power of Attorney allows you to appoint some-one to make health care decisions on your behalf should you find yourself unable to act for yourself. You will need one of these so that your surviving spouse or child can make the determination as to what to do in the event that you are in a situation where you are being kept alive artifi-cially.

DNR (Do Not Resuscitate)

This is also known as a "no code" or "allow natural death", is a legal order written either in the hospital or on a legal form to withhold CPR or advanced cardiac life support in respect of the wishes of a patient in the case their heart were to stop.

Your Executor

An executor (also called a "personal representative" in some states) is a person named in a will to carry out the wishes of the deceased person.... It is typically the exec-utor's responsibility to offer the will for probate, and funds cannot be disbursed without the approval of a probate judge.

Probation of Your Will

In simple terms, probate is nothing more than the process a legal court takes to conclude all your legal and finan-cial matters after your death. Essentially, probate is the process by which a court distributes your estate. If you've prepared a Last Will, the court will distribute according to that. Without a Last Will or Trust, the court and an ap-pointed administrator will decide how your estate will be distributed, and don't think they will do it like you would want it!

Succession

Succession is a special type of probate in Louisiana, only, and is required when there is no other method to transfer a deceased person's assets to their heirs. If someone who owns real estate in Louisiana dies while domiciled in another state, a succession will have to be opened to transfer the Louisiana property to the heirs.

Your Heirs

While you are both still living, your heirs must be spelled out very exactly and cautiously in your Last Will or Trust. Many couples want what is commonly called a "Love Nest" will, which states that the surviving spouse gets everything, and that spouse will then be the one to determine who gets what upon their death. In this type of Will, any possible heirs (children/step children) must be specifically left out of the Will, or they are typically entitled to 50% of everything the couple owns upon the death of one of the parents, which may or may not necessarily be a good thing. You may want to investigate this with your attorney, particularly if you are in a situation where there have been multiple marriages and lots of step kids involved.

Think of Your Executor

A close and well meaning, honest friend or relative is most likely your executor. Have they ever done this before?? Probably not. Take a little time to make their job easier! In the case of the "Love Nest" will, the surviving spouse would be the first executor.

They will have to take a copy of the Will or Trust to an attorney so it can be filed for probate. Preferably the attorney who wrote it for them, if they are still available. This shouldn't be horribly expensive or complicated when the first spouse passes. When the will is probated, they will be appointed as independent executrix. The clerk will issue letters testamentary, and those letters will give them the authority to act on behalf of the decedent's estate to take care of details such as:

- Insurance
- Titles to vehicles
- Credit Card and Checking and Savings Accounts
- Titles to real estate
- Your social security or retirement accounts

So ask yourself right now: do YOU know where to find all this information? If you don't, how in the world will they?? It would be wise to gather this information and keep it with your other legal documents. They will need policy number/account numbers, names of the agencies involved, any contact information possible.

So What Exactly Does the Executor Do?

The Executor will be the one to see that heirs get the things you wanted them to have, which should be listed either in the Will, Trust, or Personal Memorandum. They will also see that your final debts are paid and accounts closed out, etc. Being chosen as an executor can be both an honor and an obligation depending on the estate and the complexity of issues that arise. So a potential executor should make sure he or she knows what he or she is getting into before accepting the responsibility.

The job of executor is defined as the person named to distribute a deceased person's property that passes under his or her will, and arranges for the payment of debts and expenses. These duties apply even if a person dies without a will. In these cases, the court appoints a person called the administrator of the estate.

Here are some basics as defined by the internet:
An executor is legally responsible for sorting out the finances of the person who died, generally making sure debts and taxes are paid and what remains is properly distributed to the heirs. State law varies on the requirements of who can serve as executors, but generally, executors tend to come from the close ranks of a family—spouses, children, parents and siblings. Although state laws provide for the payment of executors, since so many executors are close family members, they often don't ask to be compensated.

In addition to carrying out duties in a diligent, impartial and honest manner, an executor may also be required to perform any or all of the following activities, among others:

- Get a copy of the will and file it with the local probate court.
  The executor is in charge of locating, reading and understanding the will—usually even if probate isn't necessary, the will still must be filed with the probate court. At this step, the executor also determines who inherits the property.

- Notify banks, credit card companies and government agencies of the decedent's death.

The Social Security Administration along with the decedent's bank and credit card companies are just some examples of who should be notified of the death.

- Set up a bank account for incoming funds and pay any ongoing bills.
  If the decedent is owed money such as incoming paychecks, this account can hold them. An executor should be on the lookout for mortgages, utilities and similar bills that still need to be paid throughout the probate process.

- File an inventory of the estate's assets with the court.
  In many states, the court requires the executor to submit a detailed inventory of the assets in probate estate.

- Decide what kind of probate is necessary.
  Because inheritance laws may facilitate the passing of certain properties without probate (such as property held jointly by a husband and wife), probate isn't always necessary. Additionally, the value of the estate may allow it to pass through an expedited process.

- Maintain property until it can be distributed or sold.
  This includes keeping up a house until it is distributed to heirs or sold—even deciding whether property needs to be sold at all. Also, an executor must be sure to find all personal property in the estate and protect it until distribution. If the decedent had a safety deposit box, the executor should locate it and keep it safe.

- Pay the estate's debts and taxes.
  State law dictates the procedure for notifying creditors, and the estate must also file final income tax returns from the first of the current year until the date of the decedent's death. If the estate is large enough, there may be state and/or federal estate taxes to pay as well.

- Distribute assets.
  Distribution occurs according to the wishes expressed in the will. If there is no will, state intestacy laws apply.

- Dispose of other property.
  If there is any property left after paying off the estate's debts and distribution to heirs, the executor is responsible for disposing of it.

- Represent the estate in court
  An executor may be required to appear in court on behalf of the estate. Since estates vary greatly in size and complexity, an executor's job may be easy or challenging to carry out—and responsibilities may very well go beyond the items in this list. But while an executor can decline the position or resign at any point in the process, sometimes all that is needed is some legal advice. Consulting with an attorney is generally necessary to make sure that the executor properly complies with his or her duties.

It's a big job! If you don't have a close friend or relative willing to take on this job, then it's customary to pay the Executor you hire 5% of your assets or a set fee you agree on in advance for taking this task on. Well worth it!

Getting It All Together

Okay so now you need to organize all this stuff and put it somewhere that's easily found when the time comes. I suggest that you get a 3 ring binder to put all your information in. It would be wise to scan copies to keep electronically in the event of an emergency or situation where you can't put your hands on the hard copy documents. I use sheet protectors to put all documents in, which keeps them nice and clean and easy to access. Another suggestion is purchasing a book on Amazon called "I'm Dead – Now What?" Quirky title but it nicely arranges all this information for you; you just fill in the blanks. It does not have a place for documents, however, so you would still need the notebook.

Here is what I recommend:
When the binder is opened, there should be front and center a page that guides the executor step by step through what he/she should do. I call it my "Big Day Planner". Here is a "generic" copy of what I have put together for mine. Yours may well be different. Again, I don't want to leave any assumptions anywhere and make it as easy as possible for the executor or whoever has to pull all this together eventually. The big thing is making sure you keep it all updated.

Note that when I refer to an "info sheet included", it is literally a copy of a bill that is owed or loan information. I have all this information in sheet protectors, because after compiling it all, you sure don't want it to get messed up or lost.

Big Day Planner
Step by Step for my Executor

Thank you so much for taking on this responsibility! I have done everything I can to make things as simple for you as possible. We had what most couples have, which is a "love nest" will. This means that if one dies, the other gets everything, leaving the last one to leave here getting to update and re-do all this stuff and make all the real decisions. If you are reading this, then we are both gone home and hopefully there's not a whole lot left to do.
****

IN THE EVENT OF AN EMERGENCY: If I am incapacitated and unable to make decisions for myself, review the health care directives I have left in the form of a medical power of attorney for finances, etc.

Statutory Durable Power of Attorney
Directive to Physicians and Family or Surrogates (DNR)
HIPPA Authorization
Medical Power of Attorney

All of these documents are necessary to allow you to make decisions for me as to my care, finances, etc. Give a copy to the hospital or personal/attending physician. A copy should be more than sufficient. These documents will give you the legal authority to make decisions for me. In the event of my death, the Power of Attorney will allow you to continue to carry out my wishes for me. You may need to present it to my bank or other places I do business with.

NOTE: Husband's documents are clipped together with a blue clip, wife's are gathered with the red clip.

If I am "clinically dead", then let me go on home. Do not keep me alive just for the sake of it.

Behind each tab in this notebook are exact instructions on what needs to be done, and the necessary papers and such you need to do it with.

Step 1, Tab/Section 1
Immediately Upon My Death

These are steps you will need to take within 24 hours of my death.

- Notify the funeral parlor who will handle my arrangements
- Name of funeral parlor/phone number:
- Be certain that you let them know that my body is to go to SW School of Medicine in Dallas and give them the letter of health information for the SW School of medicine. IF FOR SOME REASON I AM NOT ELIGIBLE FOR DONATION, THEN I CHOOSE TO BE CREMATED
- Remember to Get Several Certified Death Certificates (request a dozen copies or more)*

- See my instructions for care for my children or pets or livestock.
- Contact my place of work and let them know.
- Contact Friends/Family and Clergy using provided list.
- Check my Google Calendar and be sure any appointments I have are canceled and folks notified.
- Contact your own employer to arrange for bereavement leave.

*Death Certificate will require my birth certificate. This has to be done pronto. It is issued by the Department of State Health Services Vital Statistics. It can be ordered online or from the county clerk's office. The online address is www.tx-dps.com. The family doctor or medical examiner may provide you with this within 24 hours of the death. The funeral home may complete the form and file it with the state.

You will need the following information:
    Name of Deceased
    Date and Location of Death
    Age of Deceased
    Gender/Race/Marital Status
    Hospital/Institution in which they died
    Cause of death
    Address of Deceased
    Date and place of birth
    Name of Deceased Parents
    Birthplace of Parents
    Date and place of burial

The fee is 50.00 if you want it within 24 hours (which you most likely will), $20 if you can wait 4-6 weeks. No idea what copies cost but you should get a dozen while you are at it.

Tab 1 will contain all my vital records, contact list, letter to SW School of Medicine, and the above mentioned legal documents you will need for this step.

PLEASE DO NOT TRY TO DISTRIBUTE ANY OF MY BELONGINGS AT THIS TIME.

Step 2, Tab/Section 2
Making Final Arrangements

Within 48 hours, you will need to start making the plans for the Celebration:

I suggest you review my wishes concerning the following topics before final decisions are made:

- Memorial Services (reserve where you are going to have it; decide on date and hours)
- Obituary (what newspaper)
- Post the information regarding the memorial service to Facebook
- You will need a computer and such at the event for showing the dvd
- Check on catering for the memorial event; I leave this up to you as to what/if to even do it
- Contact special guests and remind them if they promised to sing or help with the service provide their contact info here
- Contact Clergy – provide names and contact info here

- Describe what if anything you want each person who attends to leave with. A card? A picture? Where can they be found?

Behind Tab 2 you will find the following:
    My Eulogy – to be given to clergy
    Directions for my Memorial Services including a list of honorary pall bearers
    My Obituary and Picture for it
    A DVD of Music and Pictures to use during the service

NOTE: Behind Tab 5 you will find my personal notes/letters for special loved ones. Be sure to distribute them at the memorial service; the most likely place you will see them all.

Remember to pick up any mail; note who will need to be contacted, and also be certain someone is at my home during the funeral/memorial to protect from would be thieves who would know it will be vacant for the memorial.

Step 3, Tab/Section 3
WITHIN 1-2 Weeks Later   LEGAL STUFF – OH MY!!!

Your attorney will tell you that nothing can be distributed before it goes through probate. Items which are paid for should not have to go through probate, and honestly we hope that all that kind of thing will already be done. The place and vehicles will hopefully already be distributed as we wished.

Now for the hard part. Take a copy of my will or whatever I may have to an attorney. Name here who drew up the original will. If they are not available, then use whoever you trust. You will need to take the Power of Attorney and possibly have some ID on you to prove you are really my Executor.

Locate any estate planning documents (wills or trusts), or other relevant documents such as deeds and titles. Also marriage certificates, birth or adoption certificates of children, and military discharge papers which you may need to file for benefits.

When you go see the attorney, they will need the following minimal documentation:
- Will/Trust
- Copy of deeds to any property
- Copy of any titles to automobiles, boats, trailers or other vehicles in my name that you have not already given away as to my wishes
- A copy of the Death Certificate (so you will need one asap)
- Retirement, Social Security or other income information. (Report the death to Social Security by calling 1-800-772-1213. Notify them whether the I was receiving direct deposit payments or checks. You will have to refund any money received the month of my death. Do not cash any SS checks, but return them as soon as possible. Check at 222.ssa/gov to see if there is eligibility for a $255 lump sum death benefit.)
- Copy of my personal memorandum
- A list of who I may still owe with contact information
- They will tell you what to do from there. They may need money from my account to pay debts and of course to pay THEM. Once all financial affairs are

completed, close out any bank accounts.
- Contact any insurance companies necessary, retirement plans or pensions, government benefits (SS) or other Service Providers to close accounts, collect on insurance payments, etc.
- Close any credit card accounts which may still remain in my name
- Review my list of accounts with IDs and passwords to close out whatever they are connected to, as well.
- You will need to file my taxes for me one last time. You may ask the attorney about particulars on this. I doubt seriously there will be any kind of "estate taxes".

Behind tab 3 you will find copies of all pertinent legal records as well as information on insurance, government benefits, any accounts that need to be closed and the list of IDs and passwords necessary. I will also include a copy of any monthly obligations I may have (telephone, credit card, etc) so that you have all necessary contact information.

Step 4, Tab/Section 4
Distributing My Assets
No later than 30 days after I depart:

THIS IS WHEN YOU CAN DISPENSE MY BELONGINGS AS PER MY WISHES

- Review my holdings such as property, vehicles or other sources of income and distribute or sell as per the instructions left in my Personal Memorandum.
- Cancel any memberships I may have, notify the

state DMV of my death and cancel my license.

- I will also need a final tax return. I will have noted where I keep these documents and information regarding the accountant that I use.
- Retitle any jointly held assets such as bank accounts, cars, real estate, etc.
- If there was a business that was owned, controlled, etc., check to see if there are any buy-sell agreements under which their interest must be sold.

Tab 4
Here I will have a copy of a past tax return, information regarding my accountant, drivers license, etc.

Husband/Wife
Make up one of these pages for each

The following will need to be done upon husband's departure. (If he goes before wife, then everything goes to her and will fall to her to take care of. If he goes after wife, these are the pertinents for him as well as for whatever may be left with wife's belongings/wishes, etc.)

- See his "Personal Memoradum" as to distribution of belongings.
- Life Insurance – Husband has life insurance policy – Info sheet included.
- If you haven't already, contact Social Security immediately. 1-800-772-1213. Notify them that he was receiving direct deposit payments. You will have to refund any money received the month of his death. Check at 222.ssa/gov to see if there is eligibility for a $255 lump sum death benefit. You will probably

need his SSN and perhaps a death certificate to do this with.
- Contact Work Company to cancel his retirement payments. Info sheet included.
- Contact Acme Insurance to cancel his medicare supplement. Info sheet included.
- Contact HUMANA - supplement for prescription drugs. Info sheet included.
- Don't forget about any possible military or VA bene-fits!
- Loans: Currently husband has 2 loans at Bank/ Credit Union; describe details here
- Credit Cards/Accounts –
  - Amazon - Info sheet included
- Monthly Utilities/Bills - Presently the following monthly obligations are as follows:
  - Germania Personal Auto   - info sheet included
  - Germania Home Owners Insurance – info sheet included
  - Bowie Cass Electrical Power – info sheet includ-ed
  - Windstream Telephone/Internet Service – info sheet included
  - Dish Network – info sheet included
  - Great Call – info sheet included
  - Sanitation Solutions – info sheet included
  - Trico Lumber – Make sure we don't have a bal-ance there – info sheet included
- Internet/Email
  - personal email address   password
- Trinity Mother Francis "My Chart"   ID   password:
- Vehicles:
  - Presently there are no vehicles titled in hus-band's name OR list vehicles

Step 4, Last Tab/Section

EXTRAS!! Be sure to distribute these notes and such as requested.

Moving Forward

Life is for the living!! At this point, everything should be properly dispersed. You may want to double check. Behind this tab you will find personal notes/letters for special loved ones. Please make sure you get them to those who have one.

Thank you so much for doing all this for me! I love you and will be praying that you have a happy, blessed life here on this earth, and will be waiting with open arms when I see you on the other side!

Lastly, I would suggest you strongly consider leaving a hand written note to your loved ones. Think how much that would have meant to you had your parents or spouse done this for you! Here are some other suggestions in lieu of a letter:

- Buy some "thinking of you" greeting cards you can make out to individuals and store away
- Write a poem or short story about a special event you remember with them
- Suggest they think of you when they hear your favorite scripture, which is...??
- Make a short voice recording just telling them you love them
- Buy a book or thoughtful gift to wrap and leave for them

These things would be very treasured and help them to cope with their grief, which is what this is all about! In this section, be sure your "executor" knows where these things are and to whom they are to be given! Another internet quote which is particularly appropriate here:

> "Grief, I've learned, is really just love. It's all the love you want to give, but cannot. All that unspent love gathers up in the corners of your eyes, the lump in your throat, and in that hollow part of your chest. Grief is just love with no place to go."

Your final personal thoughts and notes will help them deal with all the bottled up love….

Final Thoughts
No pun intended...

So ask yourself...... "are you between the ages of 65 and death?" The average age that an American dies is 70 for men and 72 for women. Of course there are always exceptions, but who knows?? Every day you live past 70 is a true gift! Use it wisely! When the Lord lowered our life span from around 700 years to about 120 years, it was an act of mercy! By the time I was 65, I knew from the direction I was seeing things going with man vs Satan in this world that I would not want to hang around here much longer and feel great empathy for the younger generations! This world is not my home!!

While I am sure this did not cover every possible scenario, I hope you have found it helpful and encouraging. Please take care of this responsibility. Start somewhere! There are tons of articles on the web that can help you with particulars, as well as attorneys and financial advisers. The more you know about what you want to do and what needs to be done, the easier and less costly it will be to get the legalities taken care of and your property dispersed as you would wish. If you get it all organized now, that's great, but remember you will need to update it occasionally. I would suggest you review all pertinent data every 2 years, and if your situation has drastically changed you may also want to review the legal part (trust/

will). Some states may have changes in their laws on a frequent enough basis to warrant a legal review every few years to stay current.

My final thoughts on all this: Your energy (soul) will live on without your body SOMEWHERE. That is a fact proven by science (Energy/matter cannot be created nor destroyed, only changed). That shoots a hole in the atheist theory that once you die that's it. There are two possible destinations, then. One is the "default" destination of remaining with the one who convinced you there are no alternatives and that death is final, or the other is to reject that and believe in the One who created you. You will have eternal life in one place or the other. You have to CHOOSE your creator. Since the beginning of time, man has always prized his right to "choice", and our God honors that. If you don't intentionally choose Him, then you have rejected Him. To me it boils down to that you either choose love (God) or hate (Satan), because that's what you will spend an eternity doing; either being loved or being hated. Why anyone in their right mind would reject a loving God who wants you to be able to live where He lives in Paradise for eternity is something I cannot possibly grasp. The alternative is not pleasant, to put it mildly, and once your last breath is taken, you have made the choice. Far better to die intestate than without God!

I hope this has all been of a help to you and will encourage you to get your final affairs in order but most of all make sure you know where you are going! I'll be looking for you there!

NOTES:

NOTES:

NOTES:

www.ingramcontent.com/pod-product-compliance
Lightning Source LLC
Chambersburg PA
CBHW021905170526
45157CB00005B/1982